indulgences

COFFEE & FRIENDS

Rebecca Germany

A DAYMAKER GREETING BOOK

Just as it seems coffee has been around forever, so it seems we have always known each other as friends.

Coffee is welcomed at any occasion. It's the drink that delights kings and commoners alike, and it's the thing that brings us together across a table. . .or across many miles.

So sit down and let me serve you a cup. . .

You are like

plain *coffee*...

. . .NOTHING ADDED TO THE BREW~

YOU DON'T NEED TO BRING ANYTHING
BUT YOURSELF TO THE RELATIONSHIP
AND I'M HAPPY.

In the seventeenth century, the first coffeehouses opened in London. These coffeehouses became known as "penny universities" because a person could buy a cup of coffee for 1 cent and learn more at the coffeehouse than in class!

*Good coffee
is like friendship:
rich and warm
and strong.*

TIPS FOR A GREAT CUP OF COFFEE:

- Keep ground coffees in a sealed container in the freezer to preserve freshness.

- When selecting beans to buy, the wetter they look the better the freshness and taste.

- Use ground beans immediately.

- Follow exact measurements and instructions of your brewing machine.

- Brew with fresh, filtered, cold tap water.

- Warm your mug with hot running water before filling it with coffee.

- Don't keep coffee on a hot plate for more than an hour. Keep warm in a carafe instead.

- Don't reheat old coffee.

  Don't reuse grounds.

- Clean your coffeemaker periodically with a strong solution of water and vinegar.

you are like

espresso...

...STRONG, FULL-FLAVORED COFFEE

SERVED IN SMALL PORTIONS~

YOUR ENERGY INSPIRES ME.

51% of Americans
drink coffee daily.

*Good
communication
is as stimulating
as black coffee,
and just as hard
to sleep after.*

ANNE MORROW LINDBERGH

ESPRESSO
IS THE
CONCENTRATED
COFFEE BASE
TO MANY
VARIETIES
OF COFFEE
DRINKS.

AMERICANO
1 shot espresso in a cup of hot water

BREVE
1 shot espresso with warm light cream

CAPPUCCINO
$1/3$ espresso, $1/3$ steamed milk, $1/3$ foamed milk

CON PANNA
1 shot espresso with cold whipped cream on top

LATTE
$1/3$ espresso, $2/3$ steamed milk

MACCHIATO
1 shot espresso with a dollop of foamed milk on top

MOCHA
Cappuccino with chocolate syrup

ROMANO
1 shot espresso with a twist of lemon peel

(one shot of espresso equals approximately one ounce)

Our friendship
is like *Cappuccino*...

. . .FROTHY BLEND OF ESPRESSO
AND MILK TOPPED WITH WHIPPED CREAM
AND CINNAMON~

WE ARE THE PERFECT BLEND
OF TWO UNIQUE INDIVIDUALS.

In 1686 the first café serving coffee opened in Paris—
Le Procope. . .it is still in business today!

*The glory of friendship
is not the outstretched hand,
nor the kindly smile, nor the joy
of companionship; it is the
spiritual inspiration that comes
to one when he discovers
that someone else believes in him
and is willing to trust him.*

RALPH WALDO EMERSON

INSTANT CAPPUCCINO

1 CUP POWDERED CREAMER
1 CUP POWDERED CHOCOLATE MILK MIX
$\frac{2}{3}$ CUP INSTANT COFFEE
$\frac{1}{2}$ CUP SUGAR
$\frac{1}{2}$ TEASPOON CINNAMON
$\frac{1}{2}$ TEASPOON NUTMEG

Create a fine texture to the instant coffee by putting it through the blender or coffee grinder. Combine all ingredients and mix well. Use 1–2 heaping tablespoons per cup of boiling water. Store in airtight container.

Attach brewing instructions to a jarful and give as a gift to a friend.

You are like a *latte*...

. . .A LITTLE ESPRESSO

WITH A LOT OF MILK ~

YOU BRING MUCH COMFORT

TO THE BITTERNESS OF LIFE.

Navy Secretary Josephus Daniels outlawed alcohol onboard ships. He ordered coffee become the beverage of service on the ships, hence the term "Cup of Joe."

Friendship is one
of the sweetest joys of life.
Many might have failed
beneath the bitterness
of their trial had they
not found a friend.

CHARLES SPURGEON

HONEY-NUT LATTE

1 OUNCE OF HAZELNUT SYRUP
1 OUNCE OF HONEY (OR TO YOUR TASTE)
1–2 SHOTS OF ESPRESSO
STEAMED MILK

In a large mug, mix the flavors with the espresso until honey dissolves. Fill mug with milk. Garnish with whipped cream, honey, and very finely ground nuts.

You are like
an *iced* coffee. . .

. . .BLEND OF ESPRESSO AND ICE

ENHANCED BY MILK AND FLAVORINGS~

YOUR SPIRIT REFRESHES MINE.

Coffee, as a world
commodity, is second
only to oil.

*Just thinking
about a friend makes you
want to do a happy dance,
because a friend is
someone who loves you
in spite of your faults.*

CHARLES SCHULTZ

ICED BERRY BURST

1 PACKAGE (10 OZ) FROZEN RASPBERRIES
½ CUP SUGAR
½ CUP WATER
10 CUPS COLD BREWED COFFEE
1 PINT HALF-AND-HALF
1 CUP WHIPPED CREAM
MINT SPRIGS
WHOLE RASPBERRIES

Place frozen raspberries, sugar, and water in a blender and mix until smooth. Strain mixture into a large mixing bowl, eliminating seeds. Add coffee and half-and-half and blend well. Fill chilled glasses half full of chipped ice and pour berry mixture over the ice. Top with whipped cream, mint sprigs, and whole raspberries. Serves 8–10.

You are like

flavored coffee. . .

. . .COFFEE WITH OILS AND FRAGRANCES
ADDED TO THE ROASTING PROCESS
OR SYRUPS AND LIQUEURS ADDED
TO THE BREWED CUP~

YOUR PRESENCE IS OFTEN JUST WHAT
I NEED TO FEEL COMPLETE.

Brazil produces the most coffee in the world.

Life is a chronicle
of friendship. Friends
create the world anew
each day. Without their
loving care, courage
would not suffice
to keep hearts
strong for life.

HELEN KELLER

MOLASSES AND CREAM

12 OUNCES HOT COFFEE
1 TEASPOON MOLASSES
$\frac{1}{8}$ CUP LIGHT CREAM

Combine coffee and molasses
in a large mug; stir until molasses
dissolves. Add cream and serve.

You are like *decaf* . . .

. . .COFFEE PUT THROUGH A PROCESS
TO REMOVE THE NATURAL CAFFEINE
CONTENT WHILE EITHER RETAINING
OR RETURNING THE FULL FLAVOR~

YOU'RE GOOD FOR ME.

In the year 1809, Meslitta Bentz made a filter out of her son's notebook paper, thus inventing the world's first drip coffeemaker.

A real friend
warms you
by his presence,
trusts you
with his secrets,
and remembers you
in his prayers.

AUTHOR UNKNOWN

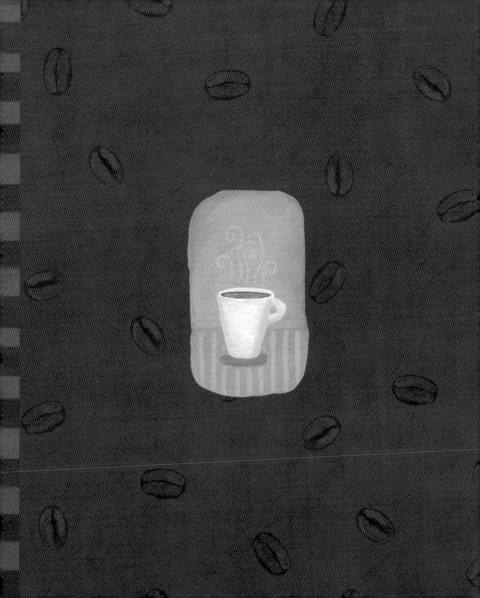

CLEAR CONSCIENCE MOCHA

In a large mug, slowly combine one
package of sugar-free hot chocolate mix
with 6–8 ounces of hot decaffeinated
coffee. Top mug with either warmed
skim or soy milk.

You are like
mocha...

. . .EQUAL PARTS OF THE WORLD'S

THREE FAVORITE THINGS:

ESPRESSO, MILK, AND CHOCOLATE〜

YOU MAKE MY LIFE COMPLETE.

It takes four thousand coffee beans to make one pound of coffee.

*A faithful
friend
is an image
of God.*

FRENCH PROVERB

CAFÉ MOCHA

Mix 1 ounce chocolate syrup and
1 shot espresso. Fill the remainder
of the coffee mug with steamed
milk. Garnish with whipped cream
and chocolate sprinkles.

I always thank my God as I remember you in my prayers.

PHILEMON 1:4

Just as I can't go long
without a mug full of coffee,
I can't go for long without you.

Let's always keep the pot
of friendship brewing.

© 2004 by Barbour Publishing, Inc.

ISBN 1-59310-199-6

Designed by Greg Jackson, www.jacksondesignco.com.

Facts taken from the National Coffee Association and www.coffeeuniverse.com.

Published by Barbour Publishing, Inc., P.O. Box 719, Uhrichsville, Ohio 44683, www.barbourbooks.com

*Our mission is to publish and distribute inspirational products
offering exceptional value and biblical encouragement to the masses.*

Printed in China.
5 4 3 2 1